29 WAYS TO BE WISE

WISDOM AND COMMON SENSE FOR EVERYDAY LIFE

Vance Richards

CONTENTS

INTRODUCTION

For wisdom is better than jewels, and all that you may desire cannot compare with her – Proverbs 8:11

Those are very strong words, what if they were even half true? Do you see many people looking for wisdom? I don't, I see a lot of people chasing after money, pleasure, comfort and other inferior things while making all kinds of costly mistakes in the process.

 I wrote this book partially for myself because I was tired of making poor decisions. I wanted to study the topic for myself, and I wanted one place I could conveniently review and reference what I learned. I've tried to make this book as concise and beneficial as possible. It's short but there's a lot packed in, so it may be best to read a bit and mull it over before moving on. It also conveniently has 29 chapters, one for every day of the month with space left for a chapter of your own insights (and a day off for months with 31 days).

These ideas are taken from my own mistakes, and wins, and of those around me, the Bible and other books, and well known thinkers and leaders. This subject is not taught in schools—it is up to you to learn it on your own. Some never learn it, some spend their whole lives making mistakes then finally learn it, and some actively pursue it, and it shows.

I hope this book is useful to you, I hope it saves you time, money, headache, and stress. Enjoy!

ALWAYS KEEP IN MIND THE FUNDAMENTALS

Success is neither magical nor mysterious. success is the natural consequences have consistently applying basic fundamentals – Jim Rohn

The fundamentals of anything you do are absolutely essential—they are the first thing you need to think about when starting something new. Let's say you want to become extremely fit and healthy—a great intention but where do you begin? Do you start by researching the latest supplements, super foods, and exercise equipment? That's like building a house by first buying the windows and door knobs—first, lay the foundation.

A logical and easy place to start would be to look at

the things you already eat and drink every day. How is the air you breathe? What else are you exposed to that might be harmful? How is the quality of your sleep? You spend a third of your life doing it. Do you move enough every day? These simple things are often overlooked in favor of the latest and greatest.

Everyone wants to skip to the fun, advanced stuff. I've notice this when playing volleyball, everyone wants to practice their jump serve or spike and it's fine and fun to try new things but none of that happens in a game without having the fundamentals firmly in place. To have a reliable jump serve you first need to be able to toss the ball to the same place consistently, and you can't be thinking about your footwork and timing while you're doing it—it has to be automatic. If you have these things in place the serve will come much easier.

If the foundation you have built is faulty or starts to deteriorate, everything you've built on top of it will be faulty as well. What is the foundation of your life built on and how solid is it? Maybe you need to go back and shore up the foundation in certain areas of your life. Keep coming back to the fundamentals again and again no matter how far advanced you get. Black belt martial artists still practice falling correctly. **Start with the basics, build on them and check them regularly to keep them solid.**

TAKE CARE OF YOURSELF

Every man is the builder of a temple called his body – Henry David Thoreau

I magine you were going to sail around the world —you only have one boat to last the entire journey. Those who do this spend a disproportionate amount of time on care and maintenance of their vessel. They are constantly checking it for wear, and protecting it from damage, they know the reason for every creak and groan. If something starts to fray, they take care if it immediately, so the problem doesn't spread. They spend the extra money for high quality materials knowing they may face storms and will need rely on the boat to perform well. Is this how you treat your body and mind? You are taking a lifetime trip in your body, spare parts are not read-

ily available, and you cannot take it for granted that others will always be there to help you. A storm will put things to the test—that's why things break at the worst possible time—so invest in yourself and keep yourself in the best shape possible.
A few things that seem to be universal are: good nutrition, clean water and clean air—it is much easier to end up with quality when you start with quality.

Mental problems are becoming more and more common. Do not neglect caring for your mind. Build a network of close friends to enjoy and to share support with. Fill your mind with joyful, grateful thoughts as much as possible, keep learning new things—use it or lose it.

This is an important principle—you can lose a lot of things in life and be ok but if you lose your health what do you have left? Whatever body and mind you have, cherish it. That does not mean don't use it, ships are made to sail but treat it like the gift that it is.

BE AUTHENTIC

Be yourself. Everyone else is taken. – Oscar Wilde

Are you being honest with yourself and others? One of the top regrets of the dying is that they lived the way others wanted them to instead of having the courage to live life on their own terms. Are you doing what you want and know is right, or are you living to please others? You don't need to be different just to be different but has your authenticity been replaced by conformity?

Do you listen to your conscience or try to ignore it? If you feel conflicted that may be a sign that you know something deep down, but you're acting contrary to it.

Have you ever acted in a certain way, or pretended you had certain qualities to please someone else? **You are uniquely you, and that's who you were meant to be.** Nobody likes a dishonest person, even when that person is being dishonest to get others to like him. That person does not even like himself when he is being dishonest about who he is.

This does not mean you do not work on yourself to improve or that you can do anything you want, at any time. There is a difference between who you are and how you act day to day. You have your own personality, and interests but you also have bad habits, flaws, and weaknesses.

You do not have to be a people pleaser to be a nice person, it's better to be good than nice anyway. You can choose to be kind, generous, and loving, but now add honest to the list. When you honour who you are instead of following the crowd, you can give your best to others.

Practice and get good at saying no. You never know when you might really need to. This can be especially hard to say to family, and close friends. Which would you rather do—say no, or overwork and neglect yourself, waste your time, and resent yourself and the other person? All that so you did not have to say no—not a particularly good payoff. Be generous, but on your own terms, **let yourself be influenced and inspired by others but not pressured.**

BE JOYFUL

A cheerful heart is a good medicine, but a down-cast spirit dries up the bones – Proverbs 17:22

What are you looking forward to? Is there anything exciting happening in your life? Life can be a boring routine if you are just going through the motions. Existing might be a better description of that than living. You will naturally work harder and do a better job at something you are passionate about. It can feel like play, and sometimes all it takes is a change in mindset.

It can be tempting to wallow in self-pity about our situations or some past mistake but what benefit does that get you? You are just reinforcing the pathway in your mind to feeling down. Snap out of it! Literally, change how you are holding and moving your body and your attitude. Everyone's situation is different, and there is a time to be somber but don't waste your life acting like Eeyore. Listen to inspiring stories and be around inspiring people. Maybe it will rub off on you. Give your mind the task of looking for the good things in your life, job, marriage etc. If your mind gets good at this, you just might turn into the most positive person you know.

Most men pursue pleasure with such breathless haste that they hurry past it – Soren Kierkegaard

Most things are better when there's fun and laughter. All things being equal who would you rather be around—a good natured optimist or a miserable pessimist? Sprinkle laughter and fun wherever you can, it will smooth out rough situations, people will like you for it, and it will even help your memory. If you can lift others up with your joy—you will be a bright spot in their week.

How do others see you? Maybe you even want to ask. We all want to be liked but are we likable? Enjoy yourself and others will too. Are you typically in a good mood, fun, generous, lighthearted or do you criticize, condemn, complain, and look for faults? **You are part of a community, and you can add value to that community simply with your joy and passion.**

UNDERSTAND YOURSELF WELL

One principle eliminates a thousand decisions –
Johnny Uzan

How well do you know yourself? What are your values and boundaries? What energises you? How often do you think about what is important to you? Could you describe yourself in three words? Sometimes it takes time and experimentation to find our answers to these questions, but they are important to figure out. Knowing yourself will help you determine what to do with yourself and let you avoid mistakes.

If you were a football team you would want to know where you are strong and weak so you could strategize accordingly. **When you know yourself well you do not need to be flawless to win because you**

know where you excel and where you do not.

If you know you're a risk taker, be extra careful if you get too excited about something. If you are naturally good with people choose a career that will develop and put those skill to good use—you will enjoy it, be good at it and be well compensated for it.

Do you know the extent of your skills and abilities? Weightlifters know exactly how much they can lift, and they don't attempt an amount that will likely injure them. It would be good to know if you could swim before jumping into deep water.

We spend our entire lives with ourselves but sometimes we do not pay attention to our strengths, weaknesses, preferences, patterns etc. Be keenly aware of what you can do, like to do, what you know, and in what conditions you best operate.

HAVE INTEGRITY

Honesty is the first chapter in the book of wisdom
– Thomas Jefferson

C an anyone be wise without integrity? The word for that might be shrewd, or cunning but without integrity long term success is doubtful—your reputation precedes you. Would you do repeat business with someone you do not trust? Starting out in the business world it is easy to believe that having high margins is the most important thing for your business. As you gain more experience you realize having trust in your suppliers is more important than high margins.

Integrity means being true to your principles, doing the right thing and being true to your word. Are you someone others can fully rely on? Can you rely on yourself? Can you be trusted with something valuable?

If someone lends you his car and you get a flat tire, get it fixed *and* washed. If they entrust you with their house, leave it *better* than you found it.

The problem is having integrity never seems to be easy to do. It even makes for a good rule of thumb, if you are struggling with a moral dilemma the harder thing to do is usually the right choice.

The good news is that if you do take the high road your good name will spread, and you will gain the respect and admiration of good people. You will be at peace with your conscience, happy with yourself and you will be inspiring others to do the right thing.

DIRECT YOUR THOUGHTS

Sow a thought and you reap an action; sow an act and you reap a habit; sow a habit and you reap a character; sow a character and you reap a destiny
– Ralph Waldo Emerson

Your thoughts and questions are powerful things, be careful not to downplay their importance. Everything begins with a thought. Everything you watch and listen to, along with your thoughts are the ingredients to your mental factory that is building your outlook on life.

Do you have poor thinking habits? Can you make a beautifully tasting feast using scraps of rotting garbage? If not, then how do you expect to make a beautiful life from scraps of mental garbage? Do not fill your mind with wars, murders, stabbings, accidents, etc. This will just lead to worry which has no benefit, in fact it can lead to health problems, which leads to more worry.

Every thought you think makes a path, think it often and the path becomes a road, and eventually a paved highway. The more well-worn the road the easier and more natural it is to go down. Decide to make living in a wonderful state of mind your default—starting and ending your day with gratitude would be a great first step. Events might be out of your control but your thoughts about them and reactions to them are not.

The Bible says it like this:

> '...whatever is true, whatever is honorable, whatever is just, whatever is pure, whatever is lovely, whatever is gracious, if there is any excellence, if there is anything worthy of praise, think about these things' Philippians 4:8

Questions are one way you direct your thoughts. **Ask better questions of yourself and you will get better answers.** Your mind will set to work answering whatever question you ask it so try asking yourself *how* you can do something, instead of why you can't.

SELF DISCIPLINE

The first and best victory is to conquer self – Plato

The ability to have control over yourself is a rare and valuable trait. You should want full control over yourself—to have the ability to keep the promises you make to yourself.

We all have a lot of 'shoulds' that we don't do anything about. We should get up early, we should exercise every day, we should put 100% effort into what we're doing. **Problems in life often come from cutting ourselves slack.** We stay up late watching videos, eating ice-cream then suffer the consequences the next day by feeling sluggish, and depressed about our weakness and expanding waistline.

You can think of self-discipline as a muscle. Maybe you have not exercised that muscle very much—start small, soon enough it will become a habit. Not only will you reap tangible benefits, but you will develop a positive view of yourself. How you see yourself is important, and self-discipline is one way to help develop a healthy self-esteem.

You can 'engineer' self-discipline to some extent. Have your exercise clothes conveniently placed beside the door ready to go. Make it harder to eat junk food and easier to eat the good stuff—put the cookies at the back of the top shelf and the fruit and veggies on the counter. Try telling others your plans to give yourself accountability & healthy pressure to do it. Be creative and you will find what works for you.

When you discipline yourself, you decrease the number of problems you have. when you do not discipline yourself, you are inviting trouble into your life, sometimes suddenly, sometimes little by little. A well-maintained tractor will actually increase in value over time and can last decades but if you do not put the effort in to take care of it, it will breakdown in just a few years.

CULTIVATE GOOD HABITS

First we make our habits, then our habits make us
–John Dryden

Essentially, once your habits are established you do them almost automatically, and without thinking. Because of this you might as well develop habits that serve you rather than hinder you. Start thinking about your daily habits, where will they take you in 5 or 10 years? Start being intentional about them and you will be being intentional about who you're becoming and where you're going.

If your habits have been making you without you realizing it, how do you change that? How do you become the type of person that rarely misses a workout? Just start, if the goal is to practice 30 minutes a day and you are tempted to miss a day, force yourself to just practice for three minutes. By doing this you will have done two important things—you will have practiced that day and reinforced to yourself that you are becoming someone that follows through on things. Plus, you may often find yourself practicing the entire 30 minutes or more simply based on momentum. Just like any action or habit, the more you do it, the easier it is to do.

HAVE HIGH STANDARDS FOR YOURSELF

If you will be hard on yourself life will be easy on you – Zig Ziglar

If you have played sports, you know when you have 'left it all on the court' and when you did not. If you did not there may be a sense of guilt that you let yourself or your team down. When you are satisfied that you gave your best effort, the results are irrelevant because you could not have done any better. You may have work to do to improve but you can have peace of mind when you lose— they were simply better. If you did not do your best, you will never know if you lost because of that little extra effort, you did not put in.

Of course, there's a time to take it easy, and if your goal is to just have fun or relax then by all means do so. If you are a chess player, I'm not saying you need to study the game to become a grandmaster. but in areas of life that matter—finances, family, health, career, character…hold yourself to being outstanding.

Be an incredible husband—your marriage and homelife may start to be a lot more smooth and fun. Be more meticulous and disciplined with your spending and you will probably find money is not as tight as used to be. Have a higher standard for your body and health and you will likely have more energy and take fewer trips to the doctor each year.

Doing your best in everything you do is one way to define success. If you are going to start something and put minimal effort into it, you might as well not bother—the results will show your lack of effort.

When you hold yourself to excellence others take notice, you will be positively influencing them without even intending to. You will be bringing out the best in others because they will feel inspired to do their best as well.

DEVELOP ENDURANCE

Victory belongs to the most persevering –Napoleon Bonaparte

Some things just take time. More skill, a better strategy, more money—none of these things will cause a tree to grow faster. You might look around and see people getting results faster than you, maybe that's true and you can learn from them. Maybe they gambled and got lucky, or maybe they have been hustling for years behind the scenes to bring them to where they are.

If you do not have patience, you will not stick with things, if you don't stick with things, you will never get good at them, if you don't get good at them you will stay a beginner, and if you stay a beginner you will be treated and paid as one.

Not everything is worth pursuing, this is where knowing yourself and what you want are important. What is a worthy goal to pursue? Start it and continue day in and day out, you will not make great gains overnight, but your results will accumulate over time or you may see no progress until one day it explodes. We all know the stories of people like Colonel Sanders who was rejected over 1000 times before eventually succeeding. It is this kind of friendly persistence that is necessary.

You also must also be consistent, if you keep stopping and restarting you will keep losing the progress you have made. Think of brushing your teeth, good posture, learning to play an instrument—these things need to be done daily not once a week.

The three traits of patience, persistence and consistency are essential if you have big goals because the payoff might be years away. Can you stay at it for that long without reward? If you can, the rewards can be great and long lasting.

BE PROACTIVE

Make it happen. Shock everyone.

Fortune favors the bold, the early bird gets the worm, find a way, he who dares wins. All these point to the principle of taking matters into your own hands, instead of waiting for something good to happen to you.

Sometimes in life you get only one chance at things. I am not advising you to be impulsive but if you are too passive or put things off, by the time you get around to the opportunity it may be gone. Sometimes you win simply because you are the only one that showed initiative, everyone else was waiting politely.

The best properties are rarely for sale, when they do get listed, they get snapped up quickly for a high price. Instead of waiting, go to the owner and make an offer. In selling they say 'ask for the sale' do not wait for the customer to tell you that he wants the product. In dating, come up with a fun idea and invite the person to join you. Do you feel like life is happening to you instead of you actively creating your life? Do you feel like you need to wait for someone or something to get started? Set your intention and begin.

You may have to risk rejection and looking foolish, and you may be alone because everyone else is scared to act—congratulations, you are being a leader instead of a follower. Do not be so passive, if you want something, pursue it. Be dogged, follow up, stay late, learn it, study it, be enthusiastic, make lots of small mistakes, ask for advice, go first, try it, start it and then figure it out. Pretend you're a wrecking ball and smash through red tape, bureaucracy, endless talk, and lame excuses—yours and others.

There is a line between reckless abandon and careful forethought. Yes, plan, but are you planning or stalling? Planning is the first step but don't forget to take the second step—doing it. Take charge, there's no calvary coming to help you or prompt you. As we get older, we start to live life on autopilot, and we ask why life is passing us by, don't let that be you.

LEARN TO BE PRODUCTIVE & EFFICIENT

You always have time for the things you put first –
Anonymous

Everyone has limited time and most of us have limited resources. It would be a good idea to use yours wisely and make the most of them. When you are productive and efficient you can do more with less. Here are some fundamentals when it comes to being productive.

Stay organized. Have you ever spent 10 minutes looking for your keys or that important note you wrote down? Staying organized will save you time and stress.

Take breaks, it is counter intuitive but if you take breaks, you will get more done. You will have more energy to pour into the time that you are working. Try resting one day a week, taking a 20- or 45-minute nap in the afternoon to recharge, or working in 45-minute periods with a 15-minute break. Not only do you get a physical rest, but your mind has a chance to reflect on and process what you are doing. You do not need to stop working if you have a lot to do—'a change is as good as a rest'.

Tackle the hardest, most unpleasant tasks first, the rest of the day will be easy by comparison. Or start with the easy stuff, build momentum and a sense of accomplishment then tackle the big things. What works for you?

*Lack of direction, not lack of time, is the problem –
Zig Ziglar*

Limit distractions. 15 minutes of high quality, focused work may be worth an hour or more of low quality, distracted work.

Use the 80/20 rule. 20% of the work will yield 80% of the results. Find out what the 20% is and do it, it may be enough for what you are trying to accomplish. Do not waste time on things that do not give a big return. The successful and unsuccessful both focus on details, just different ones.

Set a deadline—to summarize Parkinson's law—a

project will expand to fill the time you have allotted for it. Cleaning the garage will take a day or a week depending on how much time you give yourself for it.

Experiment with all these and find out what works best for you.

INCREASE YOUR KNOWLEDGE

Knowledge is power – Frances Bacon

What you don't know can hurt you, in fact people die because of a lack of knowledge.

Aim to be a well-rounded and resourceful person. This used to be more highly valued than it is today. Never stop learning and being informed, the world is constantly changing, you will need to be able to adapt to the changes.

Besides increasing your knowledge, increase your know-how with practical skills. It used to be a rite of passage that when you grew up and left the house you had certain basic skills like taking care of your body and clothes, using basic tools, holding conversation, managing money, and cooking for yourself.

You do not need a deep knowledge of most things to be reasonably competent at them. Aim to become as useful as possible and people will love having you around. Not only will your life be richer, but it will help you in other areas as well. Travel if you can, you can learn all about other places but actually going there will give you hands on knowledge like nothing else can.

You can be a master in your chosen area and also competent in many others, do this and you can be a well-respected source of advice that others will turn to.

WHAT IS THE RETURN ON INVESTMENT (ROI)?

Wisdom is the power to put our time and knowledge to the proper use – Thomas J. Watson

In poker it is called pot odds. Poker can teach you a lot about making the best decision based on limited information. It is the same skill you need in business and your personal life. You need to sort through a lot of information—to answer important questions for yourself.

Think of the games at a carnival. Before handing over your $5 ask yourself 'what are my chances of winning and if I do, how much will I win?' You might find you have a 90% chance of losing your $5 trying to win a $2 stuffed animal. This is a simple example but the principles remain for complex situations. There are opportunity costs to consider too. Spending your $5 here means you can't spend it elsewhere—maybe somewhere with better odds and prizes.

This is a big and interesting topic to study and things can get quite complicated. You need to make your best guess at the time, with partial information —you don't really know your chances of winning the game, or how much that stuffed animal is worth. Ideally **you want to risk a small amount to win a lot and have a high probability of success.**

In real life you need to decide where to invest your time, money, and energy. This applies to investment opportunities as well as it does to other opportunities in your personal and professional life.

Sometimes the best thing to do to avoid the worst-case scenario no matter what the upside might be. In poker sometimes you will not bet even when you think you have the best hand because the consequences of being wrong means lose all your chips and are out of the tournament.

People think they need to take big risks to get big rewards, that's not true, look for asymmetric risk: rewards. Lastly, don't judge the decision based on the results. Nothing is guaranteed, just because you

got a bad result does not mean you made the wrong
decision.

SEEK WISE COUNCIL

Whatever you do in life surround yourself with smart people who'll argue with you – John Wooden

This may be the best advice in this entire book. If you did this and nothing else you would save yourself much time, money, energy, and frustration. Imagine having access to decades of knowledge and experience. This is available to all of us, we simply need to seek it out. Ask someone who has been there—what a simple idea but many people will not do it because it takes humility. Are you open to hearing a different point of view? Can you admit that you could be wrong? Put aside your enthusiasm for a moment and let others play devil's advocate, let them try to poke holes in your theory and planning. A lunch with Warren Buffett sold for over a million dollars, if you can become a close friend to a wise person, you've hit the jackpot—you get to pick their brain for the price of lunch. Offer to work with & for them for free—you will likely be getting the better part of the deal. **See how they do things, ask them about their thinking, reasoning and decision making.** Look for these wise people who can help you, their lives will leave clues.

Seniors are a treasure trove of experience—they may have gone through what you are going through right now dozens of times—it's a no brainer to tap into that as much as possible. Not every senior is wise of course but you can learn from their mistakes and unique perspective.

BE PREPARED

Give me six hours to chop down a tree and I will spend the first four sharpening the axe –Abraham Lincoln

Be prepared, the Boy Scout motto. Are you prepared for the future? Is your mind prepared? Your body? Your finances? Are the people that you rely on prepared? How about your skills—are they up for the task? These are questions worth asking yourself before starting your journey or project. Just ask any baker that has had to run to the neighbor's for sugar or eggs mid-cake.

Notice the first question 'are you prepared for the future?' How can anyone know the future? **The answer is...you anticipate**. Causes produce effects. Is there a storm coming? What is the likely effect and what should I do about it? Think about the likely scenarios and problems that you could encounter. How would you react to and deal with them?

A police officer once told me when he's dealing with dangerous criminals he imagines the most likely 'what if scenarios'. 'If he charges me, I'll do this', 'if he reaches into his jacket, I'll do this' etc. Being unprepared can be inconvenient or deadly depending on the situation, many hikers have needlessly died of exposure because they went for a day hike, got lost and were not prepared to spend the night outdoors.

A lot of people do not **count the cost before they start something.** They get so excited and the picture in their head is so rosy they forget all about the costs involved, how hard it might be or what could go wrong. In short, they just do not think things through. The bigger the project the more important it is to plan ahead. Opposite to that, there is another way that people find themselves unprepared. **They are unprepared for the upside**, for the opportunity. What if things work out better than you expected? Would you be able to take advantage of it? What a shame to have customers lined up to buy but run out of product to sell them.

Even if things go perfectly and you don't end up using any of the things that you had prepared, there are two great but often overlooked benefits to being prepared—confidence and peace of mind.

USE LEVERAGE

Give me a place to stand, and a lever long enough,
and I will move the world – Archimedes

Using leverage in financial terms means borrowing money and is risky. If you borrow money to invest and you lose your investment, you still owe the borrowed money. I am not talking about leverage in the financial sense, I am talking about leveraging your time and effort.

Leverage is used in many different areas of life—think of a bicycle's gears, using levers to pry, or pulleys to lift heavy loads. In many cases you would never think of attempting some tasks without these tools. The same principles hold true in other areas of life—you do not need to reinvent the wheel or try to figure everything out yourself, someone has already done it, you just need to access their knowledge. This is where courses, seminars, tutorials, and instructional videos come in handy.

This book is a perfect example of this. Some of these principles come from big painful mistakes in my life. They also come from courses and books I have taken and read. You are benefiting from the lessons I've learned and the people I've learned from. You are hopefully avoiding countless painful errors by reading a short inexpensive book. Good for you for leveraging your time! Learn the easy way what many people have learned the hard way with their frustration, money, years and in some cases, lives. **You can learn in a few hours what took some people years to learn--this is the beauty of leverage**.

Another concept you need to be aware of is what Albert Einstein said was the 8th wonder of the world. Compound growth, normally talked about regarding money, can be summed up simply as growth on growth. The sooner you start the better because it gives you more time for the growth occur.

What is the highest leverage action you can take right now? Can you compound the growth in your business? Fitness? Relationships? Start looking for where you can use these forces in your life.

STAY IN THE ZONE

Practice does not make perfect. Only perfect practice makes perfect – Vince Lombardi

The zone is the perfect place for you to perform and learn. If you have played sports you have probably experienced it. You are totally in the moment, fully engaged in the activity at hand, time is forgotten. This happens when you are doing something in the sweet spot that is not too hard but not too easy.

Play a team that you can easily beat, and you become bored, sloppy, and learn nothing—you stoop to their level. Play a team that is out of your league and you get trampled and discouraged—learning little. But play a team that is just slightly better than you, and you are challenged and inspired. Victory is within your reach, but just barely, you must stretch and grow just a little to grab hold of it. Next time you do not need to reach as far to get to the same level—you have expanded your ability.

This applies just as well to learning new things. Do not rush, but do not go slow. Think of a video game where you are a race car driver—you want to go as fast as you can without losing control. **Only go as fast as you can think and react.**

MAKE GOOD QUALITY DECISIONS

It is in your moments of decisions that your destiny is shaped – Tony Robbins

This is a big subject and perhaps one of the hardest, but most important things to study and do. As we get older and look back at the big decisions, we've made we can see that if we had made different choices our lives could have taken a completely different path. Here are some basics to think about.

Always know your top priorities, when you keep those in mind, decisions will be easier because you simply ask yourself 'is this in line with my priorities?'

Get quality information and check your assumptions (they often go unsaid). If you base your decision on a faulty premise or bad information how good can that decision be? You need to have the warts and all reality of the situation.

Consider all your options, often we think about choosing between A&B and forget about C, D, E, F and so on. Are you dismissing something out of hand without even realizing it?

Beware of confirmation bias. We all believe certain things, when we get new information, we often interpret it based on our beliefs rather than objectively.

Keep your emotions in control, we have all overpaid for something because of our excitement, only to later come down off our high and realize what we've done. FOMO—fear of missing out—is powerful, check your emotions when making decisions.

Know why you are making a certain choice. Is fear or comfort the reason behind the choice you're making? Was it something someone said? Is it the desire to fit in? Maybe it was something you saw that you then made an assumption about. Make sure there is a good reason behind your choice.

NIP IT IN THE BUD

An ounce of prevention is worth a pound of cure –
Benjamin Franklin

Which is easier to extinguish? A candle or an entire house engulfed in flames? Make life easier on yourself—deal with small problems before they become big.

Stay on the ball in all areas of life—some ambitious people put in crazy work hours to get ahead neglecting their health, only to be forced to take time off or worse because they are suffering from something avoidable. Do not neglect areas of your life —relationships, spiritual, health, maintenance, etc. One weak link will cause the whole chain to fail. A problem could be growing out of your awareness that could be easily solved if you had just noticed it.

A good practice is to see what is coming and stay ahead of the curve, anticipate and solve problems before they even occur. If you have a newborn look ahead a few months to see what is coming your way and prepare for it now, then just take it all in stride— much better than being taken off guard and having to react at the last minute. If you hear an unusual noise while driving find out what it is before something breaks and you are left on the side of the road at the most inconvenient time. **Anticipate & prepare rather than scramble and react.**

GET GOOD AT LISTENING

Know how to listen, and you will profit even from those who talk badly – Plutarch

Being a great listener is like a superpower that you can develop with practice. It will probably come as no shock that most people are not good listeners. It takes effort and you need to be present.

We all think we listen, but we listen through filters of our own biases, beliefs, opinions, attitudes, and memories. Our minds edit, distort, emphasize, diminish, and interpret certain parts of what we hear so what reaches our brains is different from what was actually said. This is especially true in conversations about things we feel strongly about, our filters of belief, opinion, and attitude kick in. To combat this, we need to recognize when we do this and be intentional about listening without bias. Do not interrupt. Actively listen by repeating back to the person what you think they said—they will feel heard, and you will know if you have a good understanding of their message.

These three things—being present, putting aside our judgements, and actively listening are the 20% that you can do to give you 80% of the results.

You develop your superpower even more by listening for more than just the words being spoken. What is being said and what is not? Is there something being implied? Where are there silences and how long are they? Listen with your eyes to *how* it is being said—body language, facial expressions, eye movements—what is the feeling behind it? What is their tone of voice, where is their emphasis? Timing —why are they telling you this now? What is the situation and context surrounding what they are telling you? What has just happened? Can you read between the lines? Some people don't like to openly say what they're feeling, they prefer to be subtle and indirect.

Women's intuition comes from picking up on these faint emotional messages that most men miss. This type of listening will give you more information, reveal true feelings, and deception, it will also endear you to others. Listen like a detective, taking in all the clues.

BEWARE OF OVERCONFI-DENCE

The fool doth think he is wise, but the wise man knows himself a fool – Anatole France

Humility is underrated, some even see it as a weakness, but humility is simply understanding your place and is necessary for growth. Confidence is a good thing, but you need to have the right amount. Confidence comes from competence, know your limits, and push them but do not pretend you do not have any. If you're competent flying gliders, would you be fully confident jumping into the cockpit of a commercial airliner? If you have too much confidence for what you are doing you may be headed for a fall. The trouble is when you are overconfident you think you can do no wrong. When you think this way, you take bigger risks, thinking it will always work out.

We are especially vulnerable to this right after we've just had a big win. We need to be honest and objective about our skill level. Boxers and MMA fighters know the value of humility. Many learn it the hard way thinking their opponent is beneath them. Obviously, it is best to learn humility without going through the embarrassment and pain of being knocked out.

Be teachable, and open to correction, you do not know everything.

HELP YOUR TEAM EXCEL

A player who makes a team great is more valuable than a great player – John Wooden

Teaming up can be of great benefit to both parties—two cords are stronger than one and the team can be greater than the sum of its parts. Teams can also be dysfunctional and disastrous, it depends, among other things on the people involved, strategy, and communication.

We are all part of teams in our daily lives, our families, co-workers, churches, recreation groups, etc. Working well in teams requires different skill sets than working alone.

This first step is to **know the purpose and what is trying to be accomplished**. This puts everyone on the same page and allows people from the top to the bottom of an organization adapt and make decisions according to the goal.

The second step to being effective as a team is to **know you job thoroughly** and be excellent at it. This is your role in the team, if your results are lacking the whole team's result will suffer.

Next you need to **know everyone else's job and how they all interrelate**. When everyone on the team knows the purpose and process and their role in it—the team becomes very efficient. Team members can go directly to the next task without seeking clarification, they can help each other because they know what is and is not important, and what will and will not help the team.

This is where communication really comes into play, without it things can quickly descend into chaos. Often you will need to deviate from the original plan, which is fine but **the more you go off script the more you need to communicate decisions and actions.**

When it is functioning at a high level a team can be a beautiful thing—like a well-oiled machine, every piece is performing its task in harmony with others. Is your workplace that way? How about your family? Have you discussed roles? Do you know what your team members do and how you can help? Maintain your situational awareness about how you and your team are doing.

There is much more that could be said about unity,

culture, organization, strategy, and social dynamics but I will leave that for another book. Do not forget that you are dealing with other humans not machines, a little grace, appreciation, and encouragement will go a long way.

THINK CRITICALLY

Thinking is the hardest work there is, which is probably why so few engage in it – Henry Ford

Do you rely on others to do the hard work of thinking for you? Making good decisions is difficult, making good decisions based on inaccurate information is almost impossible. It is critical that you question your own assumptions and beliefs as well as what you are being told. Start with the classic who, what, where, when, why and how. If it makes sense to you—great, if not, dig deeper, there may be more than meets the eye. Curiosity allows you to uncover the truth. You find out for yourself how, why and if things work, it is a much better way to learn then just to be told. **Use logic, common sense, intuition and what you**

already know to get to the truth. It can be like a jigsaw puzzle and putting the pieces together is not always easy. Follow the evidence where it leads being curious and objective. **Uncovering the truth is about finding the best fit for *all* the evidence.**

One of the hardest things to do is question our own ideas. Do you love when people correct you? Do you look for people who disagree with you? Ask for, and carefully consider advice. Ask others to poke holes in your theory or thought process. Put on your pessimist hat for awhile, you can always put your optimist hat back on later. If you can articulate their point better than they can it means you truly understand it. You can then possibly dismiss it but you first need to hear and understand it. Objectively ask 'am I wrong?' This is the hardest part.

BEWARE OF LAZINESS

The lust for comfort, that stealthy thing that enters a house a guest, and then becomes a host, and then a master – Khalil Gibran

Watch out for laziness in yourself and others (someone else's laziness can hurt you just as easily as your own). It's a funny thing, when you are lazy you end up doing more work than if you are diligent. Don't apply yourself in school? You will end up working low level jobs, working harder than management. Be lax about taking your car in for regular maintenance? You will end up paying more to fix worn out parts. Procrastination is a special form of laziness where you work at anything else so long as it is not the thing you should be doing. It is odd behaviour really

—you do more work to avoid something that will have be done eventually. **Just start it and get it behind you as soon as possible,** the weight of it will be taken off your shoulders and mental energy will be freed up in your head.

Complacency is another form of laziness. It is characterized by sloppiness, cutting corners, and taking things for granted. Complacency has killed many people, from working at dangerous jobs to everyday things like driving.

Work hard especially at leveraged tasks—usually it takes no extra energy, but the rewards are much better. Highly value your time. As you get older time seems to speed up, do not waste it on too much sleep or entertainment. Find a worthwhile project so in 10 years, you're not just older you're older and better off somehow. **You will reap what you sow but if you sow nothing there will be nothing to reap.**

As the saying goes 'roll up your sleeves and you will never lose your shirt'. Do more than required and look for ways you can add value—you will be an asset to yourself and those around you.

LEARN FROM MISTAKES

A page of history is worth a pound of logic – Oliver Wendell Holmes

If you learn from every error you and others make in a particular area your progress will surprise you. If you do not learn from your errors, the same ones will keep tripping you up until you do. Try not to make the same mistake twice, there may not be that many different mistakes that you can make in a certain area and if you are not making mistakes, you will be performing at a higher level.

When you make a mistake do an 'autopsy' to find out what went wrong, record it so you don't repeat it. Ask others ahead of you on the journey about their mistakes—they will probably be glad to help you not make the same ones they did.

Close calls are your freebies—what did not happen but almost did or easily could have? Do not take them for granted, they are warning signs of what will happen eventually if nothing changes. Trends are another sign of things to come—it may not be a problem now but if it continues what will be the outcome?

Strive for constant incremental improvement, evaluate your own thinking and processes—that may have been where the mistake was made. Small mistakes are not the problem, they are how we learn and are expected, but avoid big mistakes that will set you back a long way.

In chess, losing your queen is a huge blow, many players resign on the spot. Others panic and impulsively make a second, often worse mistake. Instead, **regain your composure, re-evaluate, and carry on** —many games have been won that way.

BE COURAGEOUS

Timidity is the silent acceptance of bondage –
Constance Friday

Courage is necessary if you want to do anything of significance. I understand those that do not like taking risks, but the truth is – it's all risky. Getting married—you could get a divorce, having kids—they could be monsters, investing—you could lose it all, not investing—you might not have enough for retirement. The point is life is meant to be lived.

Fear of failure and rejection influences and limits your decisions, sometimes without you even being aware of it. Fear can kill an idea before it even has a chance to be tested—if you think it will fail you will not even attempt it.

Ask yourself 'what is the worst that could realistically happen?' Take a quarter of that and that's the worst that would likely happen. **Our imaginations get carried away and most of the time what we fear never even comes close to happening.** To be fair you also have to ask 'what's the best that could happen?

Is there a conversation you would like to have with someone, but you are not sure how they would react? Initiate it. If they are offended, you can offer a sincere apology and repair the damage. On the positive side you could both make it a profound insight. It may spark a deep and open discussion and a deeper friendship. It may lead to a positive change.

You need courage to live your life, you need it to love because love forgives as well as confronts. **Be cautious at times and bold at other times but never cowardly.**

THINK LONG TERM

One's first step in wisdom is to question everything
- and one's last is to come to terms with everything
– Georg Christoph Lichtenberg

The short sighted say life is too short to wait, actually life is too long not to think long term.

Some things take a long time to build so you need to think and act on them early on. This goes against our nature because the future seems so far off, we think somehow it will take care of itself. The future will not be bright by default, you need to take care of things now to establish a good future.

Top priorities must be kept top priorities. Put the big rocks in the bucket first and there will be lots of room for the sand to fill in the gaps, but if you put the sand in first there will not be enough room for all the big rocks. How often do you stop to think about what is most important to you? It is important to know what is important and what isn't. If something is important, put it on the calendar.

It is amazing that people put very little thought into the cliff we're all walking towards and eventually must face—death. Eternity is a lot longer than our lives here on earth. If you do have a soul that outlives your physical body what will happen to it? Some think we came from dust and will just return to it. Others say no one can know so what is the point in thinking about it. Some don't care to know, and some say a judgement day is coming for those not made right with God. Whatever you believe, are you sure? It is worth more than a casual thought, think deeply about it.

CONCLUSION

By now you may or may not be thinking that you have been very foolish at times throughout your life. There is good news, lady wisdom will always welcome you back no matter how foolish you have been. Start being wise today and over time the quality of your life will improve.

You can think of your life like a book, right now you are partway through the book, some are near the beginning, some near the end but whatever is already written and however much you have left, you have full control over the main character. Make him or her into the hero of your book.

No one is wise all the time, even King Solomon the wisest person to have ever lived made mistakes. Keep making progress, forgive yourself, learn and move on as you become a wiser person. Success or failure is usually not in one particular moment or decision but a series of choices and decisions.

Meditate on these concepts, see how you can apply

them in your life. Only use them if they make sense to you. These are general rules and there may be situations where something does not apply. It takes wisdom to know when, where, how *and if* to apply them.

REFERENCES